Lift off!
The Story of Spaceflight
Heather Hammonds

Chapter 1

Exploring Space

For thousands of years, people have wondered what it would be like to travel into space.

A long time ago, people wrote stories and drew pictures about space travel. They imagined what it would be like to fly to other planets.

Astronomers looked at the planets and stars. They learned a lot about space.

No one was able to send spacecraft into space. Space travel was just a dream . . .

Spacecraft are **launched** into space by rockets. In the 1940s, very big rockets were built.

Soon scientists in **Russia** and the United States built huge rockets that could carry spacecraft into space.

October 1957

Scientists in Russia launched the first spacecraft to **orbit** Earth. It did not carry any **astronauts**.

January 1958

Scientists in the United States launched a spacecraft that orbited Earth, too.

The first rockets were built by people in China around 2,000 years ago.

5

Chapter 3

The First Astronauts

We cannot live in space.

In space:

- there is no air to breathe.

- it is very cold when it is dark.

- it is very hot when it is sunny.

The word *astronaut* comes from Greek words meaning "star sailor."

Animal Astronauts

The first astronauts were animals!

November 1957

Scientists in Russia sent a dog named Laika into space. Laika was the first animal to orbit the Earth. *Laika* means "barker" in Russian!

Other animals, such as monkeys, cats, and mice, have also traveled into space.

People in Space

April 1961

Yuri Gagarin's spaceflight lasted 1 hour, 48 minutes.

An astronaut from Russia was the first man to travel into space.

Yuri Gagarin orbited Earth once. Then he landed safely back in Russia. His spaceflight made him famous.

Alan Shepard's spaceflight lasted 15 minutes, 28 seconds.

May 1961

Alan Shepard was the first astronaut from the United States to travel into space. However he did not orbit Earth.

John Glenn's spaceflight lasted 4 hours, 55 minutes.

February 1962

The first astronaut from the United States to orbit Earth was John Glenn. He orbited Earth three times!

Russia and America raced each other to build spacecraft and send astronauts into space. This was called the space race.

Travel to the Moon

The United States began the Apollo space program in 1961. Its purpose was to land a man on the moon and return him safely to Earth.

Apollo Spacecraft

The Apollo spacecraft sat on top of a huge rocket. There was a place for three astronauts to ride, live, and work. Everything the astronauts needed for a trip to the moon, including food, was in the spacecraft.

Apollo 8 mission logo

December 1968

Three astronauts traveled to the moon in Apollo 8. They were the first people to orbit the moon. However they did not land on it.

There were seventeen Apollo **space missions**. Eleven Apollo missions carried astronauts into space.

Moon Landing!

July 1969

Three astronauts traveled to the moon in the Apollo 11 spacecraft.

Two of the astronauts flew a **lunar module** down to the moon's surface. They became the first astronauts to land on the moon!

The first man to walk on the moon was Neil Armstrong. He said, "That's one small step for man, one giant leap for mankind."

The Apollo 11 mission to the moon lasted 8 days.

Learning About the Moon

Astronauts traveled to the moon five more times. They collected lots of moon rocks and took thousands of photos. They learned a lot about the moon.

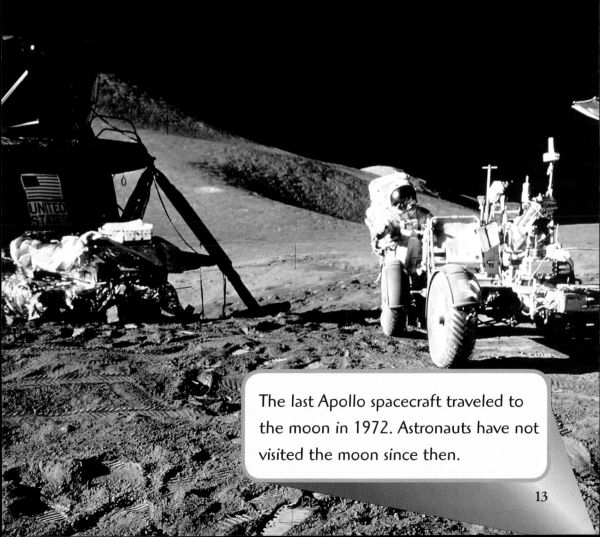

The last Apollo spacecraft traveled to the moon in 1972. Astronauts have not visited the moon since then.

Chapter 5

Space Shuttle

April 1981

The first space shuttle flew into space more than 20 years ago. The space shuttle can travel into space many times. However it cannot fly to the moon. The space shuttle orbits Earth.

NASA, a special department of the U.S. Government, has three space shuttles: Atlantis, Discovery, and Endeavour.

nose cone

crew compartment

USA

NASA
Endeavour

wings

The space shuttle flies into space with the help of large rockets and a big **fuel tank**.

The rockets and fuel tank fall to Earth as the shuttle flies into space.

fuel tank

The space shuttle is the only spacecraft that can fly into space more than once.

rockets

Life on the Space Shuttle

The space shuttle can carry up to seven astronauts. A **commander** and a pilot fly the spacecraft.

Other astronauts may:

- go on spacewalks

- work on machines that the shuttle has carried into space

- work on experiments

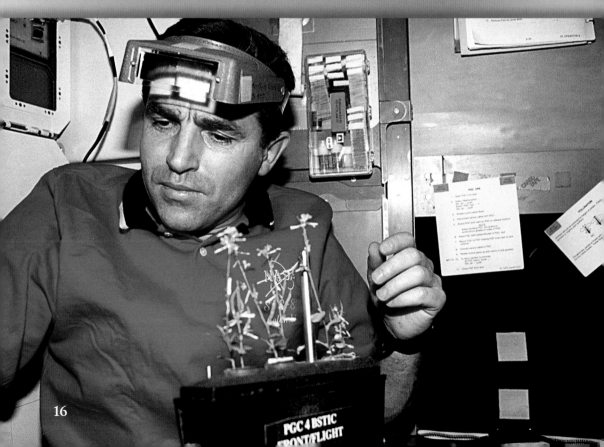

Astronauts live and work in the front part of the space shuttle. When astronauts work outside of the space shuttle, they wear space suits.

On Earth **gravity** keeps us on the ground. In space there is no gravity so astronauts float around inside the space shuttle.

Chapter 6

The International Space Station

The space shuttle is sometimes used to take astronauts and goods to the International Space Station, or ISS.

The ISS orbits Earth all the time. It cannot fly back to Earth like the space shuttle. Part of the ISS is still being built.

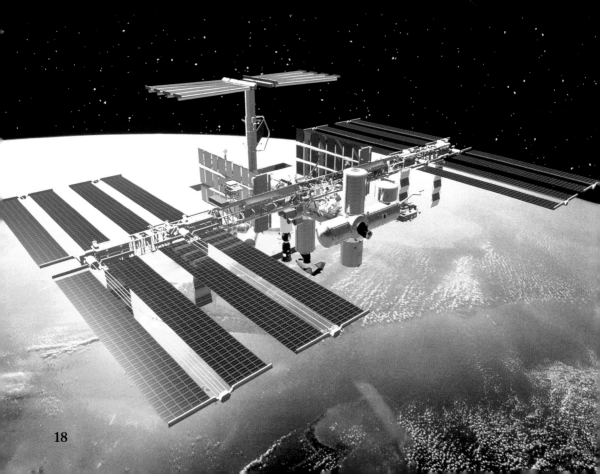

Several countries are working together to build the ISS.

Spacecraft take parts of the space station into space. Then the parts are joined together.

Russia and America built other smaller space stations before the ISS.

Chapter 7

Future Space Travel

In the future, astronauts will return to the moon. There are plans to build a base on the moon where astronauts can live and work.

Astronauts will fly to the moon in new kinds of spacecraft.

Unmanned spacecraft have been sent to the planet Mars. Scientists have learned a lot about Mars from the spacecraft.

It is hoped that, one day, astronauts will travel to Mars, too. For now only unmanned spacecraft can travel to Mars.

Unmanned spacecraft have sent back many pictures of Mars.

Chapter 8

Space Travel Time Line

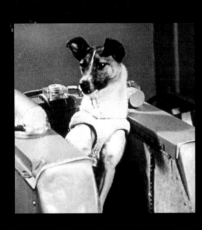

3

November 4, 1957 – Laika becomes the first animal to orbit Earth.

4 April 12, 1961 – Yuri Gagarin becomes the first man in space.

2

October 4, 1957 – The first spacecraft orbits Earth.

1

1940s – Big rockets are invented.

6 July 20, 1969 – Neil Armstrong becomes the first man to walk on the moon.

5 December 21, 1968 – Three American astronauts become the first men to orbit the moon.

7 April 12, 1981 – The first space shuttle is launched.

8 November 20, 1998 – The first part of the ISS is launched.

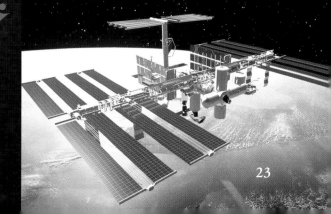

Glossary

astronaut	a member of the crew of a spacecraft who travels beyond Earth's atmosphere
astronomers	scientists who study space
commander	the leader of a group of people, such as the crew of a spacecraft
fuel tank	a tank that holds fuel, such as gasoline, to make machines go
gravity	a force that keeps everything on the ground, on Earth
launched	sent somewhere, such as into space
lunar module	a spacecraft that transports two astronauts from the main spacecraft to the surface of the moon and then back again
orbit	to circle or go around something
Russia	a large country in eastern Europe and northwestern Asia
space missions	journeys into space
unmanned	with no people inside

Index